W9-AOA-104

HOW DO THEY MAKE THAT?

PENCILS

Rachel Lynette and John Willis

MEDIA ENHANCED BOOKS
AV2
BY WEIGL™
ADDED VALUE • AUDIO VISUAL

www.av2books.com

MEDIA ENHANCED BOOKS
AV²
BY WEIGL™
ADDED VALUE · AUDIO VISUAL

AV² provides enriched content that supplements and complements this book. Weigl's AV² books strive to create inspired learning and engage young minds in a total learning experience.

Your AV² Media Enhanced books come alive with...

Audio
Listen to sections of the book read aloud.

Key Words
Study vocabulary, and complete a matching word activity.

Video
Watch informative video clips.

Quizzes
Test your knowledge.

Embedded Weblinks
Gain additional information for research.

Slide Show
View images and captions, and prepare a presentation.

Go to **www.av2books.com**, and enter this book's unique code.

Try This!
Complete activities and hands-on experiments.

BOOK CODE

F 2 8 4 8 4 5

... and much, much more!

AV² by Weigl brings you media enhanced books that support active learning.

Published by AV² by Weigl
350 5th Avenue, 59th Floor
New York, NY 10118
Website: www.av2books.com

Library of Congress Cataloging-in-Publication Data

Names: Lynette, Rachel, author | and Willis, John, author.
Title: Pencils / Rachel Lynette.
Description: New York, NY : AV2 by Weigl, [2017] | Series: How do they make that? | Includes bibliographical references and index.
Identifiers: LCCN 2016005663 (print) | LCCN 2016006698 (ebook) | ISBN 9781489645395 (hard cover : alk. paper) | ISBN 9781489650023 (soft cover : alk. paper) | ISBN 9781489645401 (Multi-user ebk.)
Subjects: LCSH: Pencils--Juvenile literature. | Pencil industry--Juvenile literature.
Classification: LCC TS1268 .L96 2017 (print) | LCC TS1268 (ebook) | DDC 674/.88--dc23
LC record available at http://lccn.loc.gov/2016005663

Printed in the United States of America in Brainerd, Minnesota
1 2 3 4 5 6 7 8 9 0 20 19 18 17 16

072016
210716

Project Coordinator: John Willis   Art Director: Terry Paulhus

Every reasonable effort has been made to trace ownership and to obtain permission to reprint copyright material. The publishers would be pleased to have any errors or omissions brought to their attention so that they may be corrected in subsequent printings.

Weigl acknowledges Getty Images, iStock, Newscom, Dreamstime, and Alamy as its primary image suppliers for this title.

Contents

All Kinds of Pencils

People use pencils every day. Young kids who are just learning to write use big, fat pencils. Small, stubby pencils are used at golf courses and libraries. Artists often use colored pencils. Have you used a pencil today?

Have you ever thought about how pencils are made? There are many steps. Take a look at a pencil right now. Look at all the different materials in your pencil. How many do you see? There should be at least three: the part that writes, the wood around it, and the eraser.
The first step to making a pencil starts in the forest. That is where the wood comes from.

A single pencil can write more than **45,000 words** or draw a line **35 miles** (56 kilometers) long.

Colored pencils are made in a wide range of different colors.

Incense cedar trees can grow to be as tall as 195 feet (60 meters).

How Do They Make That?

In the Forest

Most pencils are made from incense cedar trees. The wood from these trees is perfect for pencils. It does not break easily, but it is soft enough to sharpen. It also does not split or shrink in hot or humid weather. Many people like the smell of cedar wood. Can you imagine the smell of a newly sharpened pencil?

Incense cedar trees grow in central and northern California and the southern part of Oregon. These trees are grown in **sustainable** forests.

Along with pencils, paper is another product that is made from wood.

Foresters are workers who manage the forests. They plan when trees are cut down and make sure that new trees are planted. That way, there will always be new trees growing.

Incense cedar trees are cut down using chainsaws or large machines. The trees are loaded onto trucks and taken to sawmills. About 300,000 pencils can be made from one large incense cedar tree.

Some kinds of pencils are made from recycled blue jeans.

The Sawmill

At the sawmill, sawing machines are used. These machines cut logs into pencil stock. Pencil stock are long blocks of wood that are cut to the same size. When they are made into pencils, very little wood is wasted. The pencil stock is dried in a special kiln, or oven. It removes moisture from the wood. Now the pencil stock is ready to be loaded onto trucks or trains to travel to the slat factory.

Sawmill saws are shaped like a circle. They turn at high speed to cut logs into smaller pieces.

It is important for pencil slats to be the same size, so that the pencils will fit together properly.

The Slat Factory

At the slat factory, the pencil stock is cut into smaller blocks. They are called pencil blocks. The pencil blocks are 8 inches (20 centimeters) long. Next, a circular saw is used. It cuts each block into several very thin pieces, called pencil slats. The slats are treated with stain and wax. This makes the wood all the same color. It also makes the wood easier to work with and sharpen.

Now the slats can be shipped to pencil factories. Often, the slats travel by truck or train. If the pencil factory is on another continent, the slats may be loaded onto ships. Slats that come from trees in California may be shipped all the way to China or Germany to be made into pencils.

At the Pencil Factory

The outside of a pencil is important, but the inside is even more important. The inside is the part that does the writing. It is called the lead, but it is not made from lead. The inside of a pencil is made from a soft **mineral** called **graphite.** At the pencil factory, powdered graphite is mixed with clay and water to make a soft paste. The paste is pushed through narrow tubes. This forms it into spaghetti-like rods. The rods are cut into pencil-length pieces. Then they are baked in a very hot oven. Now the leads are ready to be put into pencils.

The heat from the oven makes the graphite hard and smooth.

There is still some work to be done before pencil leads can be put into pencils. When the wood slats get to the factory, they are run under a giant cutting wheel. The wheel cuts six to nine shallow grooves into each slat. The grooves are filled with glue by another machine. Next, a third machine places leads in the slats. A second slat is coated with glue and laid on top of the first slat. This is done with a machine called a lead layer. This makes a kind of sandwich with the two grooved slats and the leads in the middle. Finally, the slats are put between two clamps. The clamps press the slats together while the glue dries.

A shaping machine cuts each slat two times. These cuts shape and separate the pencils. The first cut is on the top of the slat. It makes half of the hexagon shape of a pencil. The second cut is made on the bottom slat. It forms the other half of the hexagon. When that second cut is made, the slat separates into individual pencils. Not all pencils are hexagons. Some pencils have round sides.

Today, machines do most of the work when making pencils.

Now, the pencils are checked for quality. The lead might not be in the center of the pencil, or the wood may be chipped. A worker sharpens one pencil from each batch by hand. This tests the quality of the lead. Then the tip is tested for strength. The pencil is held in a clamp while a plunger presses on the tip until it breaks. A machine measures how much **pressure** the tip can take before it breaks. If it breaks too soon, the pencil is not sold.

Most pencils are shaped into hexagons. This shape keeps them from rolling off desks.

FABER-CASTELL

FABER-CASTELL

FABER-CASTELL

FABER-CASTELL

It is important to test pencils. This makes sure that a pencil will sharpen and write correctly.

The next step is to paint the pencils. To paint the pencils quickly and evenly, workers run the pencils through a machine. It coats the pencil in paint. A pencil needs at least four coats of paint. Some pencils are coated with paint up to eight times. A final clear coat of **lacquer** is added at the end. It seals the paint and makes the pencil tough and shiny.

Next, a machine stamps each pencil. It marks the name of the company that produced it. It marks a number that tells how hard the lead is. You probably use a number 2 pencil for most of your schoolwork. Artists often use soft leads. You may have also noticed the letters "HB" on your pencil. HB stands for "Hard Black." It tells you that the lead inside the pencil is hard and black.

Harder leads have more clay mixed into the graphite. Softer leads have less clay.

Most pencils have erasers at the top. The eraser may be made at the same factory that makes the pencil. It may also be shipped from a factory that only makes erasers. Pencil erasers are called plugs. Plugs can be made from rubber or **vinyl**. To make the plugs, the raw ingredients are mixed together and heated. In addition to rubber or vinyl, plugs may contain vegetable oil, **sulfur**, **pumice,** coloring, and other **chemicals**. Then, the mixture is forced through a small hole in a machine called an extruder. The mixture comes out of the hole in a long, thin strand. The strands are cut into 3-foot (1-meter) pieces. If the strands are made from rubber, they must be heated for the rubber to **cure**. Vinyl does not need to be cured.

Next, a machine cuts the strands into tiny plugs. Thousands of plugs are then dumped into a giant drum machine. It spins slowly for several hours. As the plugs tumble against each other, their edges rub together and become rounded.

Erasers were attached to pencils for the first time in 1858.

Now the eraser can be attached to the rest of the pencil. A machine is used to do this job. There are several steps. Can you see the band of metal on a pencil? That metal band is called a **ferrule**. It holds the eraser in place. The pencils move down a **conveyor belt** to the different parts of the machine. Each part has its own job to do.

The first part of the machine squeezes or cuts the edges of the top of the pencil. This makes it smaller than the rest of the pencil. Then a plunger slides a ferrule over that end of the pencil. Some pencil factories use glue to keep the ferrule in place. If glue is not used, the ferrule is squeezed onto the pencil. Next, the machine places an eraser into the open end of the ferrule. If glue has been used, a plunger pushes the plug into place. If glue has not been used, the machine crimps the ferrule.

Machines crimp the ferrules to keep the erasers from falling out.

With the eraser in place, the pencil is finished. However, some pencils are sold already sharpened. These pencils are sharpened using a grinding drum. The pencils are rolled across the drum at an angle. This makes the tips touch the drum. When the pencils reach the end of the drum, the pencils have perfect points.

Now the pencils are ready to be put into boxes. Machines or people put just the right number of pencils in each box and seal it. The boxes are put into larger boxes and loaded onto trucks. They are taken to warehouses until it is time for them to be shipped to stores.

Every year more than 14 billion pencils are made in the world. Two billion of those are made in the United States.

Pencils and their boxes may be certain colors to show what kind of pencil they are.

Students use colored pencils for art projects and number two pencils for taking tests.

Into Your Hand

You can buy pencils at office supply stores, supermarkets, and variety stores. You may even be able to buy them at your school. Most pencils come in boxes, but sometimes special pencils are sold individually. Have you ever bought a pencil with a purple star eraser? Do you have one with your school's name on it? These extras do not come from the pencil factory. Another company adds them later.

You need pencils for tests and schoolwork. Maybe you like to sketch with them. Having a pencil is always a good thing. Just remember to bring your sharpener, too.

Quiz

Match the steps with the pictures.

A. In the forest

B. At the sawmill

C. The slat factory

D. Pencil lead made

E. Erasers added

F. Into boxes

Key Words

chemicals: substances made using chemistry

conveyor belt: a moving belt that takes materials from one place to another in a factory

cure: to treat something with heat or chemicals to make it last longer

ferrule: a metal band that is used to connect an eraser to a pencil

graphite: a black or gray mineral that is used as leads in pencils

lacquer: a liquid coating that is put on wood or metal to make it shiny and hard

mineral: a material found in nature that is not an animal or plant, such as gold or graphite

pressure: a force that presses on something

pumice: a light gray rock used in erasers and other products

sulfur: a yellow chemical that is used in rubber and other products

sustainable: Something which can be kept going or growing, such as a forest

vinyl: a light and very strong kind of plastic that is used to make products

Index

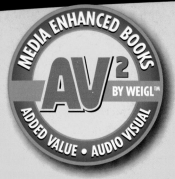

Log on to www.av2books.com

AV² by Weigl brings you media enhanced books that support active learning. Go to www.av2books.com, and enter the special code found on page 2 of this book. You will gain access to enriched and enhanced content that supplements and complements this book. Content includes video, audio, weblinks, quizzes, a slide show, and activities.

AV² Online Navigation

Book Pages
AV² pages directly correspond to pages in the book.

Key Words
Study vocabulary, and complete a matching word activity.

Quizzes
Test your knowledge.

Slide Show
View images and captions, and prepare a presentation.

Audio
Listen to sections of the book read aloud

Video
Watch informative video clips.

Embedded Weblinks
Gain additional information for research.

Try This!
Complete activities and hands-on experiments.

AV² was built to bridge the gap between print and digital. We encourage you to tell us what you like and what you want to see in the future.

Sign up to be an AV² Ambassador at www.av2books.com/ambassador.

Due to the dynamic nature of the Internet, some of the URLs and activities provided as part of AV² by Weigl may have changed or ceased to exist. AV² by Weigl accepts no responsibility for any such changes. All media enhanced books are regularly monitored to update addresses and sites in a timely manner. Contact AV² by Weigl at 1-866-649-3445 or av2books@weigl.com with any questions, comments, or feedback.